TEN WAYS
TOP SALES REPS
ARE DIFFERENT

By Duane Lakin, Ph.D.

www.LakinAssociates.com

ISBN 978-0-9679162-8-6   ©2015

Preface

Everybody wants to have Top Sales Reps. But few managers understand what makes them tick. They are different, and they need different management attention. This book is about Top Sales Reps—sales professionals who are consistently top performers.

This book does NOT answer the question, *"What does it take to be a great sales person?"* You probably have seen hundreds of lists and books that try to answer that question. It is likely that most Top Sales Reps have many of the characteristics posted in such lists, but having many of those characteristics does not mean the person is a Top Sales Rep. Ask any Sales Manager.

Few managers understand Top Sales Reps. Top Sales Reps have needs and concerns that are different from what is found in average sellers. What a manager might say to an average sales person could be seen as insulting by a Top Sales Rep.

Managers need to know what makes Top Sales Reps different. What do they have in common? What motivates them? What offends them? How can I best help them be successful? How do I know if my sales candidate is a Top Sales Rep? Should I promote my Top Sales Rep? What do I do when I see my Top Sales Rep is in a slump?

What, then, is found ONLY in Top Sales Reps? What makes Top Sales Reps different? How do you find them and care for them? That is the focus of this book.

I have worked with Top Sales Reps for over 30 years, and I want to share my observations with you. In this book, I describe what makes a Top Sales Rep different. I also offer <u>interview tips</u> and <u>management tips</u> to help you find and care for your Top Sales Reps. I hope you find the book useful.

Duane Lakin, Ph.D.
Lakin Associates

Chapter One:

INTRODUCTION

Not all sales jobs are alike. If you look at the jobs that are called "sales", you will see that some are order-taking jobs. Some include delivery of the service or product. Some are one-time sales while some require maintenance of a relationship. Some require a seller who can speak knowledgeably about highly technical details, while others require creative selling of intangibles.

To be successful in any of these sales jobs, the individual must meet the job requirements for that specific situation. Perhaps some can be "challengers" while others need to be "missionaries". Every sales job has unique characteristics that must be respected. What determines success in any specific sales job is job specific.

Therefore, it should not be surprising to hear that not all sales people are alike. They don't look alike or sell in the same way. When test sellers want to "profile" your top performers to build a model of the traits that will create success for you in future hires, they are often very successful...at selling tests.

Try this: Take your top sales producers and put them in a room. Do they look alike? Do they dress in a similar way? Do they sound alike? Do they have similar interests? Are they all extroverts? Are they all verbal?

Probably not!

Any group of Top Sales Reps is more likely to include more individual differences then similarities on the sur-face. It is only beneath the surface that you can begin to under-stand and see that a Top Sales Rep thinks in a unique way when compared with an average producer.

Yet writers are constantly telling us "Fifteen things that make a sales person great!" Then we see a list like the fol-lowing:

> Positive self-image (confidence)
> Passion
> Integrity
> Ambition
> Dependability
> Gregariousness
> Empathy
> Energy/Persistence
> Hunger for money
> Comfortable talking about money
> Assertiveness
> Durability

Ego strength
Positive attitude
Hard working
Thick-skinned

Lists like this may tell us what characteristics are needed to succeed in sales. They might make good checklists for interviewing sales candidates. But these characteristics do not really show us anything that is unique about Top Sales Reps—those who are consistently high producers in any setting.

If you look at the above list, you will see great ideas about what a seller needs to be effective. *But some weak sellers may also have these characteristics.* Haven't you seen an average seller who is still confident and committed? Many average sellers are sociable, friendly, outgoing. Any seller who has sold for more than two years has to have learned to be thick-skinned. And if a seller doesn't have integrity, he/she will not last long in any setting. "Hard working" seems obvious as a success requirement, yet I have known Top Sales Reps who do *not* work particularly hard. They work *smart* but not necessarily hard. How about "Positive Self-Image?" I have seen Top Sales Reps who have awful self-image issues, yet they can put on a mask in a sales situation and appear confident and assertive. These lists are interesting, but they do not tell us much about Top Sales Reps.

Psychologists talk about the "Big Five." These are traits that describe people and represent five independent dimensions: Neuroticism, Extraversion, Openness, Agreeableness, and Conscientiousness. Yet, these "super-traits" do not tell us much about sales people, especially Top Sales Reps. In fact, most research has found that only Conscientiousness helps predict work performance in general.

So what does it take to be a great sales person, a Top Sales Rep? It depends. It depends on the sales job and the environment. And in fact, the magic formula is not known.

The basic problem with these lists is that they are a list of traits and attitudes that sound good. Probably many Top Sales Reps have most of these traits. But so do a lot of *average* sellers.

But Top Sales Reps actually do things differently. They see the world differently. And they often do the right things for reasons that may not necessarily correlate to an assumed trait. Just looking for a list of traits in a candidate can be misleading.

Traits help us describe the dynamics that make up the personality of a person. They can sometimes help us understand a person's potential as well as inherent limitations if not addressed. Absent or missing traits can be as important as positive active traits in helping us to under stand observed behavior. (If a person is missing "integrity", it can explain a lot of observed behavior!)

Behaviors are more prone to change or to react to the environment than are traits. If a trait is strong enough, it can drive a behavior. But we cannot always know which is the driving trait. Even when looking at a specific behavior, you cannot always be sure what is driving it. The seller who is confident and assertive in the way he/she talks to a prospect may be driven to that behavior by insecurities rather than ego strength, for instance.

The only way to understand a behavior is to ask questions of the person doing the behaving. Why are you doing that? What are you saying to yourself? This is the basis of "modeling", an approach to understanding others that is much stronger than test profiling but also much more time consuming and requires a skilled investigator.

In order to understand Top Sales Reps, it is necessary to understand the behaviors that are occurring and what is driving those behaviors. Top Sales Reps have "drivers" that may not be easily seen. Understanding those drivers can help a Sales Manager do a better job of looking for Top Sales Rep candidates as well as helping a Top Sales Rep continue to excel.

It is unusual for someone to move in a linear fashion from being an average seller to being a Top Sales Rep. Being a top-producing sales rep is more than just developing new skills and learning the product/service. Top Sales Reps are different. Their behaviors are different. Their motivation and drivers are different. Average sellers may have some of these same characteristics, but they will not have all of them. When you *interview* for a Top Sales Rep, you need to look for different things and ask different questions. When you *manage* a Top Sales Rep, you must manage with an understanding of their differences and needs. They are a different animal. Choose and care for them carefully.

So what makes a Top Sales Rep different? Some things are drivers, some are attitudes, and some are behaviors. But when combined, they describe most Top Sales Reps. The following characteristics and the way they impact the seller's behavior are what make a Top Sales Rep different:
    Fear/Anxiety
    Short-term focus
    Need to feel in control
    Grit
    Curiosity
    Assumption of success
    Use of plans and mental re-plays
    Social intelligence
    Referral requests
    Use of mirroring

Chapter Two:

FEAR/ANXIETY ("MY LUCK MAY HAVE RUN OUT")

Top Sales Reps act confident. They are not.

> *When working with Dean Witter many years ago, I was told the story of a senior manager who took his top two producers to breakfast one day. He said, "You both make well over a million dollars a year. Yet you are both the first ones in each morning and the last to leave at night. Why? I want you to write as simple an answer as you can on the back of this piece of paper." He gave them a moment and then took the papers from them. Both had written the same word: FEAR*

Top Sales Reps can appear arrogant and superior at times. But beneath the surface, their driving force is fear. They are anxious that their string of successes will run out. They fear that they are lucky, and any day, that luck may run out. As a result, they must work harder each day to prevent such failure.

> *The #1 seller with the food distributor John Sexton & Co. (owned by Beatrice Foods at the time) had come within $50 of breaking the all-time sales record for a fiscal year. I stopped by his desk to congratulate him. I mentioned how close he had come to breaking the record. He just laughed and opened his bottom desk drawer. In the drawer, he had thrown a stack of papers. I indicated that I did not understand.*
>
> *He said, "Those are orders I did not turn in this month. I was afraid I was just getting a lot of end-of-year orders, and I would have no sales at all in January. So I tossed the orders in here until after January 1." In his drawer were at least $500 worth of sales orders.*

Most Top Sales Reps will not admit to fear. But listen to their words. They often talk about being "lucky." "Lucky" means they believe it could all end tomorrow. When asked to explain what they do that is different from others, they will grasp at concepts that only sound good but reflect little of what they do. They rarely can tell you why they are successful.

"Lucky" also means "I'm not sure I can do it again." As a result, it is often the Top Sales Reps who yell loudest about having their quotas increased. A larger target for the next year, based on their performance for this year, only increases their fear. They typically sandbag their forecasts, not just to ensure that they will get their bonuses, but as a way of dealing with their fear about their future.

> *I once heard a sales manager complaining about the lack of urgency in a sales rep. The manager had been a Top Sales Rep before being promoted. Her complaint: "This may be the only time we have such a window of opportunity with this customer."*
>
> *Logically, this is not likely to be true. However, she is a Top Sales Rep by nature, and her fear is that such an opportunity could disappear. It is not "We have an opportunity and let's move on it." Instead, it is "We have an opportunity and may lose it."*

12

Top Sales Reps could be classified in psychological terms as "Away-from" personalities rather than "Toward." They want to prevent or avoid failure. That is why, as Daniel Pink has observed in a recent book, incentives do not really work with top performers. Top Sales Reps are motivated to prevent failure, and a quota with bonus is nice but not a driver. Their drive is internal and comes from their need to avoid that which they fear the most—failure. If they do not get their bonus, they are disappointed and even angry, but the real reason is that missing their target suggests that failure may be lurking ahead. If they achieve their bonus, it is enjoyed, but it does not motivate them to do anything different the next year. It is also why some Top Sales Reps, when they get in a slump, have more difficulty than most crawling out of it. Average sellers may see a slump as temporary. Top Sales Reps assume it is their worst nightmare coming true.

The fear I see in Top Sales Reps is what I call a "healthy neurosis." It is the reason they answer the phone quickly, yell about orders being slow to get through the office, or complain that customer service is not being responsive to a customer need. When a neurosis becomes so bad that a person is afraid to act, then it is no longer a motivator but a liability. But a *healthy* neurosis is seen as an excellent source of motivation. It drives the Top Sales Rep to work hard the next day rather than relax after a big sale. After all, today may have been the result of luck, and tomorrow may begin a long drought of no-sales. Therefore, they get up early and tackle the job that needs to be done.

Top Sales Reps lack "ego strength", a trait often listed as a requirement for sales success. The term "ego strength" usually means confidence, tenacity, and thick-skinned tolerance for rejection. What they have instead is *ego incompleteness*. Their egos are not complete until they can conquer something, sell something. And once they get a win, they immediately worry about whether they will be able to get another one.

Top Sales Reps often act as if they have great confidence. But they don't. Their egos are fragile and need validation that they are going to be successful and not fail. A Top Sales Rep looks strong and confident when the sales are coming in, but that façade quickly fades when sales dry up.

Top Sales Reps have egos that are weakened by their own fears. They fear they will run out of luck, and they fear that they may not be able to control enough of their world to stay successful. In the end, they are haunted by the question they ask themselves: *Am I good enough?*

An "incomplete" ego makes the Top Sales Rep want and need to make the sale for a personal or ego-enhancing end, not merely for the money to be gained or for a sense of achievement. They have to make the sale to give them

14

some peace of mind. The sale—the conquest or sense of control—validates their importance and their power.

Their energy and drive is *not* ego strength; it is the result of the *lack* of ego strength that pushes them forward.

The need to fill or validate the ego is a driver that leads Top Sales Reps to act in a highly competitive fashion. Their behavior is competitive. But this is not the same as being "achievement oriented." They want to compete to fill *their* need. They are not necessarily seeking a specific achievement. Sure, their boss gave them a quota, but they are not really motivated by that number. Instead, they set internal goals that are rarely spoken or even consciously recognized. They are probably short-term. They just know they need to win—today and tomorrow--and they may make virtually any activity into a competition.

With Top Sales Reps, their self-assessment is often nega-tive. Selling helps them fill the hole that is somehow in-side them. They may feel the need to compensate for something in their life or past, and success as a seller does the trick.

With some Top Sales Reps, their self-assessment may be less negative, but still there is something missing. Influ-encing others feeds the hunger for attention or validation. You may have met Top Sales Reps who talk as if they are invincible and have all the answers. It is highly unlikely that the person actually believes the act. Top Sales Reps do not feel complete, and they need to have their ego supported. Managers need to understand this and ignore the occasional blustering and bragging that can be part of the office patter.

The need to feed the ego is a powerful source of internal motivation. This motivation always takes precedent over any external motivation. Trips, awards, bonuses, or prizes are always appreciated, but they do little to motivate Top Sales Reps. They march to their own music, and the tune is one that says, "Fill me. Make me feel important to me." As David Kahle wrote in his blog,

> *The best salespeople are beyond the reach of all these programs of exterior motivation because they march to the beat of an internal drum, an inherent hunger for success no matter what the circumstances. It's that internal motivation that lights the fire that distills all the other qualities. And that drive to succeed is far more potent than any of the other qualities. Given a strong internal motivation, I believe that sooner or later the individual who is driven to success will succeed. It's only a matter of time.*

Interview Tips:

I often ask,

> *"Do you see yourself as lucky?"*

If, *"Yes, sometimes"*, ask the candidate to talk about a situation seen as being an example of being lucky. Then follow-up with the question,

> *"Do you ever worry that your luck will run out?"*

Keep in mind, most Top Sales Reps will deny their own fear, so you may not get "lucky" comments. Listen, however, for hints in their review of their work that suggest that they worry about succeeding and fear failing. Ask,

> *"How did you get that sale?"*

> *"Why do you think you were able to do that?"*

These questions can sometimes reveal "lucky" comments.

If you believe you have a lot of rapport, you can ask,

> *"What are you afraid of? What worries you?"*

Listen and see if you get some recognition of their own insecurities.

"How do you get past the fear?"

This question may lead to comments about working harder and being diligent. That is a good sign that you might be talking to a Top Sales Rep. If you get, *"I guess I just don't let it bother me,"* then you may not be talking to a Top Sales Rep. Remember, Top Sales Reps will usually deny they have fears, so avoid over-interpreting one or two comments during the interview. Listen carefully for trends.

Management Tips:

Because they have fragile egos, Top Sales Reps are easily offended. They are sensitive to slights. They are easily insulted and irritated. They do not do well with a manager who criticizes without acknowledging their successes. Top Sales Reps need to know their boss notices them.

While a quota target is not necessarily motivating to a Top Sales Rep, behavior can be impacted by a simple posting of results. If a Top Sales Rep does not see his or her name near the top, he/she is likely to respond with more drive and determination. To slightly distort an old joke, sometimes it is not important to outrun the bear but only to outrun the other campers. Top Sales Reps want to be the best...even if the "best" is only 50% of the quota. Want to inspire a Top Sales Rep? Hire another Top Sales Rep.

But sometimes such posting of results can backfire. Top Sales Reps can lose their drive on occasion. Their doubts will overwhelm the drivers. A long string of no-sales will eat at anyone's confidence eventually. *("See, I knew my luck would run out. I'm through.")*

The manager must intervene when a Top Sales Rep is in a slump and help find a way for the seller to win again. It will not take much. A win...and the drive returns. Sometimes this means being a bit more lenient in pricing or how a deal is structured to help the seller "win." It is a short-term fix, but short-term is usually sufficient to start the engine again for a Top Sales Rep. Avoid letting the person indulge in prolonged self-pity. Self-pity can be a wave of negatives that builds and builds. Intervene quickly. A motivation speech is not needed. Instead, help them get a win. Remember, Top Sales Reps already assume their luck will soon run out. A string of no-sales, and they will begin to believe their greatest fear has suddenly come true. The manager cannot talk a person out of this thinking. Instead, help the person score a win, and the fear will get back to a level that can be managed and be a positive force rather than a negative one.

Top Sales Reps have pride...they don't need trophies or plaques. They are self-motivated. They expect to be the best, and they are competitive. In anything they do, they have pride. That is, they set a standard, compete with themselves, and feel good about meeting their own standard. This can be the best burger maker in the restaurant, the fastest bundler in a box factory, or the lab rat with the cleanest bench area. They have pride, and they show that pride in the way they compete, even if they are only competing with their own personal goal.

Top Sales Reps need to know that they are making more money than the average seller on the team. Cash bonuses and raises may not motivate, but they will keep you from losing that Top Sales Rep to a competitor. In today's world, every member of your sales team is on the Internet and probably still has a resume posted somewhere. If a Top Sales Rep feels someone else is getting the same or more pay, he/she will take those calls from the recruiter.

Fairness is very important to a Top Sales Rep. If a Top Sales Rep is given an unusually difficult sales region or territory, he/she will resent it unless there is some way to compensate for the challenge. Top Sales Reps need to feel everyone is on equal footing, and then their skill will

20

be noticed and will yield rewards. They demand a fair playing field and a chance to be the best.

Chapter Three:

SHORT-TERM SCOPE OF FOCUS

One additional reason that quotas and goal targets are not motivating to Top Sales Reps is due to their short-term scope of thinking. They do not look very far ahead. They talk about tomorrow or, at best, the end of the month. They are not inclined to worry about next quarter or the end of the year.

If you want to "motivate" a Top Sales Rep, design a compensation formula simple enough that he/she can compute how much was made *today*.

I knew a young woman who once sold text-books for a publishing company. I asked her after her first trip to the Northwest, "How much did you make?" She had no idea. And she really was not interested in finding an answer to the question. She had done well, she felt, and that was sufficient.

She was the number one salesperson in the company that quarter. And she never sold again. She was transferred into an editor role soon after our conversation. She was not a Top Sales Rep. Selling was not in her DNA. She measured her value in an entirely different way, and her manager was wise enough to recognize that fact.

Top Sales Reps worry about tomorrow. At best, they may worry about next month. They protect themselves for the short run. They do not focus on the end-of-year goal. Instead, they worry about results for this day or maybe this week.

Top Sales Reps look for efficient answers to problems. They are not interested in strategy. They want the shortest distance possible between the customer and a signed agreement.

They can often lose sight of the bigger picture at times. People may accuse them of being self-focused or selfish, of not being "team players." This is not true. They are focused on short term, specific results. And results they can control. This is why they are inclined to act independently and forcibly at times. They simply are pushing to get the result they want. Today.

INTERVIEW TIP:

Ask the candidate,

> *"When you start a new month, what are you thinking about?"*

It is doubtful a Top Sales Rep will talk about the department's goal for the year. If you get an "interview" answer, like, *"I think about how to help the team meet our goals,"* then ask,

> *"What is your team goal?"*

They probably cannot answer that question in much detail.

> *"How, specifically, does that team goal impact what you do that first day of the month? And the next day and next day after that?"*

> *"How do you change your approach to fit that team goal?"*

> *"Give me an example of where you changed your sales approach or plan due to a team goal."*

24

It is unlikely these questions will make sense to a Top Sales Rep. The Top Sales Rep will only be planning for his or her next trip or call. He or she will do as desired, regardless of the goals for the team.

Ask about individual (rather than team) goals and see if you get a different response, one that is probably short-term in focus.

> *"What is your selling goal right now? What are you working on today?"*

MANAGEMENT TIP:

Top Sales Reps are short-term focused. But a manager must think about the month, quarter, and year at the minimum. The manager must consider different approaches and options to reach that goal. Often there is a need for a Plan A and a Plan B.

The manager, therefore, must *translate* those ideas into specific short-term directions for the Top Sales Rep. The team or manager's goal will largely be meaningless to a seller if it does not translate into some clear direction for the next few weeks for that specific seller. The goal primarily provides a context for what he/she is being asked to do. Explain the overall goal. Then help the sales rep focus again on a his/her specific short–term contribution that will help accomplish the larger goal, the outcome that the manager needs to build toward success for the longer term. Talk the sales person's language—short-term and specific.

Chapter Four:

NEED to FEEL IN CONTROL

Top Sales Reps fear their luck will run out. To manage that fear, they develop a strong need to feel in control. They believe that if they control enough factors in the sales process, they decrease their risk of failing. They are able to tell themselves that they are preventing the problems that will hurt them.

Anyone who has worked with a Top Sales Rep has seen this need to control. As soon as an order is submitted, the sales rep will be calling to see the progress on the order. He/she will be checking with production or the warehouse to ensure that the product will be available as promised. Although sales managers want their sellers in the field talking with customers, Top Sales Reps often spend much of their time trying to control the internal sales ordering process. It is not unusual for a sales manager to suddenly see a Top Sales Rep wandering the halls of the office or filling emails with questions and follow-up requests for status reports.

When you ask a Top Sales Rep what he/she wants in a sales manager, you will often hear this control issue. As a recent candidate told me, *"I want a manager who can be a resource to work with finance or production to be sure that things get done."*

A recent sales model referred to as The Challenger Model describes a seller as someone who wants to debate and push the customer. While this is not wholly inaccurate, it seems to miss the real point of the behavior. The Top Sales Rep will push and advise only when he/she sees a need to step in and control. As long as a Top Sales Rep feels in control, he/she will not push. There is no need, and the risk of being seen as pushy is too great. Knowledge that can be shared and the ability to lead the customer to trust the seller's judgment result in the control a Top Sales Rep needs. He/she does not have to be entertaining, assertive, or pushy. A Top Sales Rep does not have to "challenge."

It is common to see the trait "gregariousness" on the list of "must-have's" for sellers. If you want to be a successful seller, you need to be friendly, sociable, outgoing, and gregarious, the pundits say. *Experience says this is not true.*

Top Sales Reps are not necessarily friendly and outgoing. They are often less sympathetic than many sellers and certainly more controlling. In spite of what many popular lists may suggest, Top Sales Reps are not apt to be overly concerned with others. Rather than having empathy, their primary focus is how others or other situations impact them. They are often slow to trust others. Some are even introverted in non-selling settings. Often they may not be seen as the friendliest people in the building. They may keep to themselves and avoid socializing with the other sales people in the office. If you look for "outgoing" as a requirement during a hiring interview, you run a risk of getting someone who is socially motivated which is very different than someone who needs to control. Haven't you seen the friendly, outgoing person who socializes but may not sell? Socializers often resist the risk of offending someone by insisting on a price, for instance. Socializers believe a sale happens while you are busy helping a customer by answering questions or looking up information or when taking a prospect to ball games; they don't embrace the need to sell and influence and control.

Socializers run a risk of enjoying the interaction with a customer or prospect and forgetting that they are there to sell.

> *I was once asked to work with a group of inside sales people who handled hundreds of calls a day per person. The problem was that the time spent per order kept growing. The sellers enjoyed talking with*

*the customers and wasted costly time, be-
cause while they were talking, other potential customers were on hold. They
needed to find a way to STOP being so
friendly!*

A Top Sales Rep will be quick to dismiss a prospect if he
or she feels the meeting is a waste of time. One of the ad-
vantages of experience for a Top Sales Rep is that he/she
will see when to stay and build a relationship and when
to walk away. Top Sales Reps qualify prospects very
quickly. They don't need to socialize. They need to gain
control and get a sale. If they see no hope of a sale, they
exit.

Top Sales Reps don't worry about closing techniques.
They control the process long before it is time for a tradi-
tional close.

*A Top Sales Rep for a restaurant service
company has a clever way to control the
typical close resistance. As he discusses
price with the prospect, he laments that
his boss will give him a hard time if the
margins are too low. He then (figuratively
or literally) gets on the same side of the
table as the prospect and asks, "How can
we put together a deal that will satisfy my
boss?" It is clever and has helped him be*

a Top Sales Rep in the company for many years.

Top Sales Reps know it is not the customer who needs to be controlled. It is the *PROCESS*. The Top Sales Rep learns how to control the sales process, which includes influencing the decision to make the purchase, knowing who needs to be involved, "selling" the sales manager on the deal, controlling the order processing, keeping watch over customer service, and checking that the order is delivered correctly. This is why Top Sales Reps often create havoc in an office by looking over others' shoulders and stepping on toes in an effort to get an order processed quickly and accurately.

Top Sales Reps want control. Control gives them peace of mind. Some control with an assertive approach and skilled verbal behavior. Some control in more subtle ways. But in the end, they are in control of the process.

Interview Hint:

When interviewing a sales candidate, one of the first things to look for is how effectively the candidate tries to control the interview. Top Sales Reps are able to stay "on message" in spite of attempts to distract the candidate. They are polite but focused. They may refer back to an earlier question by saying, *"You were asking earlier about…"*, for instance.

31

The Top Sales Rep candidate also may not be eager to engage in small talk. The stereotype of the sales candidate who references the fish on the wall or the photo of the family skiing is misleading. The top sales candidate will stay focused and want to talk about his/her sales successes in the past as well as why he/she would be a great fit for the company doing the hiring.

Management Hint:

Top Sales Reps are often disruptive in an office setting. They are the ones who go into the plant to find out what is holding things up or fail to fill out expense forms, because they hate paperwork. They don't want to use SalesForce.com or any other CRM system, because it is reporting and they are not in control.

Sales managers often make a mistake when they become inflexible about how they manage. One wise sales manager started doing the proposal entries for a Top Sales Rep, in part to get them done, but also to send the clear message: I want you selling and not spending time with this paperwork. On the other hand, I have seen managers who will refuse to look at a proposal until the proper electronic recording is complete. If a Top Sales Rep can demonstrate that his/her time is best spent with customers and not entering data into a CRM, why fight it? If a manager feels he or she must control the sales representative, who's problem is that? In fact, one reason Top Sales Reps don't typically become top sales managers is this very reason.

Top Sales Reps need to control. If they become sales managers, their need to control becomes problematic. Top managers need to let Top Sales Reps control…and sell. Simplify the internal system, if necessary.

Chapter Five:

GRIT

It takes energy to sell. Any good seller is motivated to get up and go to battle. But for the Top Sales Reps, it is different. They have more than energy. They have more than "motivation." They demonstrate "grit."

Angela Duckworth is an assistant professor at Penn. She has been studying "grit" for many years. She defines it as "sticking with things over the very long term until you master them." A person with grit has more than energy. He or she has stamina and determination.

A Top Sales Rep with "grit" wants a goal badly enough that working toward that goal is not work but just part of the process. An average seller, for instance, is willing to make cold calls but may complain about it and find other things to fill the day when possible. A Top Sales Rep who needs to make cold calls to sell will look upon the activity as just another thing that has to be done. It is not separate from the goal of being a good seller and meeting sales goals. It is one and the same.

*A recent candidate told me about getting a job with one of the largest chemical companies in the world. He said his first two months were spent in what they called Sales Boot Camp. About a third of the people left before the training was complete, either of their own choice or because they were asked to leave. He said it never occurred to him that he might not finish. It was hard, but it was **what was necessary** to get the job and excel.*

Many people have goals. But how many never let go of them? As Duckworth says, graduating from a two-year school is a challenge, but it is nothing like graduating from a four-year college. It usually takes "grit" to hang in and go through all the academic hurdles, pay the price, and forego other activities to get the four-year degree.

In spite of Duckworth's example, a college degree...or the absence of a college degree...does not, by itself, lend any clues about "grit." Does getting a degree online require as much "grit" as getting a degree in a conventional academic setting? It depends. It is not the degree; it is what it took to get it. That is how you find out about "grit." The candidate who told me recently that he is thinking about getting his college degree does not *have "grit", at least in the area of academic achievement. Thinking about doing something is not all that tough.*

But the person may have "grit" in other areas of his/her life. Academic "grit" is not a pre-requisite to being an achiever in the work world and in sales. But the successful candidate must show some "grit" somewhere in life that is meaningful. If the person has "grit" somewhere, it is up to the manager to ensure that such "grit" is brought into the sales job.

A Top Sales Rep must have "grit" to meet quotas and excel. It helps to be smart and driven, but it is focus and persistence that characterize "grit."

Athletes often have "grit", and their stories give a hint about what to listen for when interviewing in search of a Top Sales Rep. " *You gotta want it so bad you are willing to be exhausted*" was how one football player described college pre-season. Vladimir Horowitz, the esteemed piano player, hated practicing, but he practiced four hours a day, because that was what it took to be great. A former Pro Bowl player in the NFL said, "*Sure it hurt, but I knew it was worth it*" when describing the exercises and drills he endured every year of his playing career. A Navy SEAL described his experience in this way: "*It was the toughest training I ever experienced but I knew it was necessary."*

"Worth it"? "Necessary?" These words only make sense when paired with a clear focus, even obsession, toward an end goal. To someone with "grit", the end goal is so important that whatever it takes to get there is worth it. Necessary. No complaints. No skimping. No sneaking out of practice or finding excuses to not make calls. The goal is clear and the steps to get there are simply part of the process.

"Grit" is character. Character differentiates good sellers from Top Sales Reps. People with "grit" do not give up. Nor do they complain. They do the "reps" and run the steps and study the financial reports and hit balls out of the sand and play scales. They do what they must to reach their goal of being excellent. Some say it takes 10,000 hours to excel at something. Those with "grit" are not keeping track of the time.

"Grit" is a habit. Top Sales Reps are apt to have a history of demonstrating grit in any activity that they value. They may have hobbies that require enormous detail or attention. They are apt to have a history of persistence and refusing to give up when challenged.

I knew one Top Sales Rep in a basic commodity business that spent his evenings reading esoteric academic tomes. He was a student and scholar of ancient philosophies.

Another Top Sales Rep had been an outstanding baseball player and had been scouted by the pros since age 12 until getting hurt in college. As a teen, he would spend 16 hours a day in the summer working on various aspects of his game including hours in his garage at night practicing hitting a ball to improve his left-handed batting. When an injury forced him to leave baseball and take a sales job, he became a Top Sales Rep immediately. He had "grit".

"Grit" is often paired with "passion." When someone is passionate about something, he/she is often willing to accept the associated costs. Top Sales Reps are typically passionate about *something*. However their passion may not always be about their actual job. However, the presence of "grit" in their nature will show in other aspects of their life as well as their work practices. Competitiveness, passion and "grit" create a set of habits that are not limited to the work setting.

For Top Sales Reps, they do not think about how hard it is to do something. They simply have a habit of giving their all to what interests them, even if it may be unpleasant. It is the end that is important to them, and the means are simply part of the journey.

INTERVIEW TIP:

Remember, Top Sales Reps tend to have a short-term focus in the way they look at selling. The idea of a goal worth pushing for may not be seen in a sales context. But they often have real goals for their life or family or hobbies. And they may have "grit" when it comes to being better than anyone else at something. Look for "grit" in areas that may or may not include selling.

When interviewing sales candidates, ask "grit" questions. Ask the candidate,

> "What have you wanted so badly that you gave up other things to achieve?"

> "Was there ever anything so important to you that you suffered through things others might have called boring or hard or even impossible? Describe what you endured. Why did you do that? (Listen for the goal.) Why was that so important to you?"

"What was the most difficult learning experience you ever had?"

"What was the toughest challenge you ever faced? How did you overcome it? Why did you go to so much trouble?"

"Tell me about something you wanted to master but had to really struggle to reach that level."

"What are you passionate about? How hard have you worked at it?"

MANAGEMENT TIP:

Find what is important to your seller. Then link that important value or outcome to the sales task ahead. Help the seller see that short-term sales results can lead to the outcome he/she wants. Make selling relevant to the person's larger goal(s), and you can help that person stay focused. If there is focus and relevance that connects to the person's passion, motivation will not be an issue, assuming the person has "grit."

Chapter Six:

CURIOSITY

Top Sales Reps approach a sales call from a perspective that is different from average sellers. Top Sales Reps are thinking about what they need to *learn*, while average sellers are thinking about what they want to *say*. Therefore, it is not surprising that a Top Sales Rep does far more listening and asks far more questions during a sales call than an average seller. Top Sales Reps are thinking about what questions they want to ask to learn what they want to learn.

Average sellers are thinking about what questions the prospect may ask of them! The average seller is drawing on experience and knowledge to be prepared for the customer's questions. The average seller is focusing on being prepared and demonstrating personal competence.

The Top Sales Rep is thinking about what he/she wants to learn in this call to help accomplish the goal. The Top Sales Rep is curious. The goal is well-defined, and the pre-call thoughts are about what questions to ask and what information to look for to move the process forward.

Top Sales Reps know the power of knowledge. Information gives them confidence and an increased sense of the
control they seek. As a result, they are always looking to
see what they can learn that will help them achieve their
goals. They ask questions and they listen.

> *A food ingredient company had been supply-
> ing the lab of a major food processor for several
> years. The sales people worked closely with the
> R&D lab where new formulations were being
> tested. One day, while leaving the lab and
> walking through the main production floor, a
> new sales person on the team asked, "Isn't that
> tomato soup?" "Yes, of course," he was told.
> "That is our biggest seller."*

> *It turns out that tomato soup needs yeast, the
> primary ingredient sold by the food ingredient
> company. But for two years or more, no one
> had ever asked what else the customer made
> and would there be other opportunities to sell
> them additional products. They had simply
> gone to the research lab and sold small orders
> of their products. Until a new sales person–a
> potential Top Sales Rep–joined the team, no
> one was curious enough to look around and
> ask about other applications.*

Top Sales Reps are curious. They ask questions. They truly want to know. They are interested in what is around them and what they can learn from others to help them have an advantage. This curiosity can sometimes take the form of competitive intelligence gathering, such as reading a competitors invoice that was accidentally left on someone's desk. Just as often, it is an active and conscious effort to ask questions and learn more about a customer as well as a market. It is not surprising, perhaps, that there is a program called "Question-Based Selling." Top Sales Reps ask questions.

But these questions cannot be canned. They can't learn "Five Questions to Ask Your Prospect." True curiosity is not just an attitude. It is a *habit*, and a passion…a drive for new information. Top Sales Reps are not looking for answers. They are looking for insights and information. *They ask questions and listen to the answers.* Top Sales Reps want to know what the prospect worries about and wants to achieve. What problems does the prospect have? What is a typical day like for the prospect? What help does the customer need? How does the prospect want to be sold?

The questions that are important to a Top Sales Rep are not "qualifying questions". They are not part of "consultative selling", a process that can test the patience of some buyers. The typical sales process where a sales person asks about needs or current vendors or similar "checklist" questions does not provide what Top Sales Reps want to know. In fact, such questions can seem like an interrogation and can be off-putting to prospects and to Top Sales Reps.

Top Sales Reps want to know who the prospect is, what is important to that person, and how is the best way to influence and make a difference to this individual. What is the business and where is the pain? Who are my competitors? Who is influential in making decisions in the business? What is your wish list? These are more broad-based than "How many pounds of nitric acid do you use in a month?" These are things she can learn by listening and observing, not by following a checklist of questions. These are not answers to questions she has to ask because her sales manager requires them. These are answers he wants to discover to satisfy his curiosity and to give him an advantage.

It may be because of their curiosity that Top Sales Reps are good listeners and, often, good conversationalists. They often have a broad knowledge of topics and issues, and because they are always learning, they can talk intelligently about many different topics. Still, *it is their ability to listen that most correlates with their success in sales*. It is hard to sell value if you do not want to listen and learn.

Curiosity also fits well with the competitive drive of Top Sales Reps. Simply put, they want to know more than the next person. They want to know how someone else can sell or make a change, and they use that information to make themselves more competitive and successful.

Another key correlate of curiosity is the Top Sales Reps' relative comfort with ambiguity. Few average sellers are comfortable outside the lines of what they expect and know and are accustomed to seeing. Top Sales Reps are not afraid of ambiguity, because they are curious. They want to know more. They want to understand and find clarity. Average sellers want to get back "on script" and talk about what they planned to talk about.

> I had a salesman from Pitney Bowes come to my office one day. I wanted to ask about a piece of equipment I had found in the closet left by a former tenant. I wanted to know if it worked.
>
> The salesman entered the office, shook my hand, and announced, "I can save you $200 a month in postage."
>
> I was a bit fascinated, since he had asked no questions about why I had asked him to come or even how much postage I was currently us-ing. Had he asked any questions, he would

*have learned that, at that time, I was not
spending $200/month in postage.*

Top Sales Reps not only plan a call in a way different
from average sellers, they *leave* a call in different way.
Top Sales Reps leave a sales call re-playing the interaction in their head. They are thinking about what was said
and what they could have said in a different manner.
They are learning from their experience, even if they
failed to achieve their goal. Every interaction becomes a
learning experience. Average sellers typically are thinking
about what they need to do next or where they need to
go now that the sales call is concluded.

Curiosity does not typically equate to wanting to participate in "sales training", however. Top Sales Reps are curious about ways to reduce their fear and the risk of failing with useful knowledge and information. While curious and motivated to learn what will give them better
control and influence, they are *not* eager to participate in
formal learning situations. They are skeptical. They are
also fearful of looking foolish or stupid in front of their
peers. Typical training programs are painful to most Top
Sales Reps.

Still, they will be curious and learn enough to use a new
skill when they need it to win their goal. Top Sales Reps
expect to win, and they know when they are not winning.
Average sellers may not notice when a sales call is going

poorly, but Top Sales Reps will. They have the determination to stay engaged and involved until they are successful (if possible). As a result, if they are aware of a new option or a new way to make a proposal, they will often be one of the first of their peers to try it. While not showing a lot of enthusiasm for the training *per se*, they will draw from that training when they need it.

> *The President of a small manufacturing company was a participant in a workshop on psychological selling skills. He was largely unimpressed with the program, because he believed he was a very successful seller and did not need to do the work needed to learn some new skills. In the participant survey, he did not rate the program very high.*
>
> *The next week, he was making a sales presentation. Unfortunately, it was not going well, and he knew it. As he described it later, "I didn't know what to do, so I tried one of the crazy things Lakin was talking about last week. All of a sudden, the room changed, and I got my price without any real pushback or negotiation. I would like to change my rating that I gave that presentation last week. It was definitely a '10'."*

Trainers should not expect Top Sales Reps to be enthusiastic participants in a training session, unless they can incorporate competitive games into the learning process. Yet Top Sales Reps are often the first to test a skill in the field and report results back to the others. But they will only use the skill when existing skills are not working for them and they ask themselves, "What else might work here?" Learning for the sake of learning will not motivate them.

Learning must contribute to their sense of control over a situation when failure is suddenly a real possibility. When there is a chance they might fail, they will learn and use anything that is seen as a possible way to give them a competitive advantage.

The desire to learn means that the best Top Sales Reps are also apt to be intelligent. Intelligence measures often correlate with success in sales. Unfortunately, some smart sellers lack the other characteristics needed to be a Top Sales Rep. But every Top Sales Rep will likely score well on intelligence tests. Top Sales Reps gather data, and they know how to analyze that information. Such analytical thinking requires intelligence and education in how to engage in critical thinking.

Top Sales Reps are smart, and this intelligence adds depth and value to their curiosity. They know how to find and use relevant resources, and they are driven to find the best options toward a solution. This requires intelligence and critical thinking skills. Socializers will ask questions to "feel the pain" of the prospect, and such "empathy" is often on the list of traits needed to be successful in sales. The difference is that the Top Sales Rep is asking questions to help find the best path to solve the problem for the prospect and make a sale. Empathy is not the issue. Curiosity and a drive to learn, understand, and provide a solution is what makes a Top Sales Rep different.

INTERVIEW TIP:

Notice if the candidate is asking questions. Curiosity should be evident in an interview. Also, ask questions such as,

> *"What is the most interesting or surprising thing you have learned from a prospect?"*

Then ask,

> *"How did that insight help you make a sale?"*

Listen for an answer that is relevant.

Look and listen for evidence of the candidate's intelligence level. Is he/she providing evidence of some critical thinking? Can she/he sort out useful information from random data?

> *"How do you decide what is most important when you talk with a prospect?"*

Listen for evidence of sound thinking.

Ask about their recent experience with "sharpening the saw", as Covey would call it. Ask,

> *" What have you done to learn new skills or insights to help you be more effective?"*

> *"What are you doing better today than you did two years ago?"*

> *"Where does "continuous improvement" fit in your professional life?'*

MANAGEMENT TIP:

Help the seller identify what has been learned and assist in the sorting process following a sales call. Often you may learn something that can be useful to others on your sales team. Also, share information you have that might be relevant to the Top Sales Rep. Be an additional information resource.

Ask questions that the Top Sales Rep may have failed to consider. Be careful to avoid making this sound as if you are criticizing. Instead, emphasize that such a question might be useful in the *next* sales call the seller makes.

Prior to a call, ask the seller what he/she wants to learn? *"How will you approach this? What are you going to be listening for?"* Help "prime the pump" before the sales call.

Chapter Seven:

ASSUMPTION OF SUCCESS

Top Sales Reps expect to be successful. When they make a sales call, they assume they will leave having made some progress or a sale. They assume they will get what they wanted from the interaction. As one Top Sales Rep said, *"I don't intend to leave without an order."* Simple. Clear. Success is expected.

This is more than "optimism." It is more than just confidence that a solution can be found. It is *determination* and *expectation* that a result will be achieved.

By assuming success, a Top Sales Rep is not thrown by a "no." A rejection simply means that a workaround is needed. There is another path that needs to be taken to get the expected success. To a Top Sales Rep, a "no" is simply an invitation to get creative.

Although their scope of thinking tends to be short-term, their focus is strong. They have a strong sense of what they are trying to get and the direction they need to take. Some may call this "achievement orientation"; others may call it persistence or drive. Whatever the label, Top Sales Reps know what they want and expect to get it.

Top Sales Reps make this assumption partly due to their belief that they are more competent than most people. They do not necessarily believe they are smarter, but they do believe they are more skilled at selling than anyone else. Managers who ignore this self-image will only discourage a Top Sales Rep. Giving advice to a Top Sales Rep must not include sales tips, unless the tips are unique and are part of a training program for everyone. Top Sales Reps do not want to be coached on how to sell. Instead, they want to be given special support, VIP handling of their orders, and permission to bend the rules at times.

The "assumption of success" leads to Top Sales Reps being more flexible than most sellers. They will change direction quickly, even act impulsively at times if it seems to move them closer to what they want. For many, they will stay in motion, believing that as long as they are moving, they will eventually find themselves accomplishing their goal. Such flexibility and energy are part of the reason Top Sales Reps are often first adapters of new ideas or techniques. While they may resist the training process, they will try anything when a situation is not under their control. They will try "new" things but only when "old" things are not working for them. They expect success, and they will stay flexible until they get it.

Top Sales Reps, by definition, are typically successful. When they experience a failure, they are likely to put it out of their minds and move forward. Some may learn from the experience, but most simply concentrate on the next opportunity. As one manager once described a Top Sales Rep, *"If he sold a product that blew up and destroyed the customer's plant, he'd be back the next day offering to sell a product to the customer to help clean up the mess."* Some describe this trait as "fearless." In reality, it is a defense mechanism that enables Top Sales Reps to forget about a setback and anticipate success again.

Consequently, they have little experience with prolonged failure or disappointments. As a result, when Top Sales Reps hit the inevitable dry spell, they have few internal resources to handle the anxiety. An optimist simply expects to find a solution and eventually overcome the bad luck. A Top Sales Rep has no idea what has gone wrong and no idea what to do to solve the problem. An "assumption of success" is *not* optimism. Therefore, when that dry spell hits, Top Sales Reps are stunned. Their confidence tanks, and they can go into a negative spin. They stop trusting themselves, and they stop trusting others. They can even get a bit paranoid and start wondering who is undermining them.

Managers must move quickly to stop the negative spin. Find a way to make a sale with the Top Sales Rep and avoid taking the credit. Give sure-fire leads to the Top Sales Rep.

Pep talks are not going to work. Only a new success will help the Top Sales Rep begin to believe that he/she can again assume success with the next call or opportunity.

INTERVIEW TIP:

Ask the candidate,

> *"When you are about to call on a new prospect, what do you expect to happen?"*

> *"Give me a specific example."*

A Top Sales Rep is likely to respond, "I expect to be successful."

It also can be helpful to ask a candidate to describe a particularly successful sale, one where the seller had to overcome a lot of obstacles.

Ask,
> *"Why didn't you give up? What kept you pursuing this sale?"*

Top Sales Reps will give an answer that indicates it never occurred to them that they might not be successful.

MANAGEMENT TIP:

As mentioned above, avoid offering sales *advice*. A Top Sales Rep does not want to hear it. It is likely to make him/her angry or defensive. Instead, when a seller gets down, find a way to find a win. A Top Sales Rep does not need to be told how to ride a horse. He/she only needs to be helped to get back in the saddle. Give Top Sales Reps a win, and they will be back in the race.

Sometimes Top Sales Reps talk themselves into a dry spell. They change their pre-call planning and begin saying negative things to themselves. These "limiting beliefs" can seep into a seller's mind and cripple him/her. A manager may overcome this problem by helping the seller rehearse the pre-planning. Ask, "What are you thinking about?" "What do you want to accomplish?" "What is the key thing you want to learn in this call?" "How will you know when you've learned it?" By helping the seller return to the practices that have helped in the past, you can re-start the success engine.

Chapter Eight

USE OF PLANS AND MENTAL RE-PLAYS

Average sellers think differently before and after a sales call. Their behavior may appear similar, but their thinking processes are different.

The average seller, before a call, is thinking about what he/she wants to say. Support material and similar resources are reviewed and packed. The focus is what the seller plans to do, how something is to be said, and how to "sell" the prospect.

Too often, average sellers are thinking as much about what their sales manager tells them to do as they are about the prospect. *Am I asking the right questions? Am I following the process to qualify the prospect? Am I filling in the report sheet as I go? How can I find out when their service contract ends?*

In contrast, Top Sales Reps are thinking about what they want to learn. They are thinking about the questions they want to ask and answers they want to get.

Their questions are guided by their clear objective for the call. They know what they want to accomplish. They also know that any objective will require inquiry and learning. They need to learn as much as they can about the person or people they are meeting. *What is the prospect trying to accomplish? What are the goals the company gave the prospect, and how can I help him/her meet those goals? What obstacles is the prospect facing, and how can I help?* These kinds of questions, fueled by a clear call objective as well as true curiosity give the Top Sales Rep a different approach to a sales call.

Top Sales Reps also display a keen sense of social awareness. They are alert to how someone acts, and they are prepared to adjust their presentation accordingly. As they approach a sales call, Top Sales Reps anticipate whom they are going to see and how to adjust their interactions to fit the person they are meeting. Even when the CRM does not ask for such information, Top Sales Reps are reviewing in their heads the individual characteristics and style of the people they are preparing to meet.

After the call, differences are again seen between the average sales representative and Top Sales Reps.

Average sellers often put a sales call quickly out of their minds. They leave someone's office and begin thinking about their next call or what they want to do next. One reason many sellers resist using CRM's is their reluctance to think about a call once it has been made. They are ready to move on. They may see little value in revisiting a call in their minds.

Top Sales Reps, who may be just as resistant to CRM's, leave a sales call replaying the call in their heads. *What went well? How did he/she react to my comments? How could I have approached the issue differently with better results? What do I need to remember for the next time we meet?*

Top Sales Reps are also more likely to recall promises made. Their follow-up is more instinctive than simply good sales discipline. They would not consider *not* following up. To Top Sales Reps, follow-up is as vital as the call preparation.

Top Sales Reps are natural replay experts. They replay the call and learn from the process. While they do not have what the NFL calls "Coaches Films" to review, they have their memory and their perceptive awareness of what they did and what they may want to do differently next time. For this reason, Top Sales Reps do not typically make the same mistake twice.

INTERVIEW TIP:

Ask the candidate,

> *"When you are about to make a sales call, what are you saying to yourself?"*

> *"In the parking lot or just before you make a call, what are you thinking about?"*

> *"Tell me about a sales call you made last week...what did you learn from it?"*

> *"If you could make that call again, what would you do differently?"*

Then ask the candidate to tell about *another* sales call he/she made in the last week or ten days, asking the same set of questions. Hint: Each time, require the candidate to be specific and name the person they called on. This prevents general answers that can be rehearsed prior to the interview.

Ask questions to help you determine if the candidate is learning and replaying the sales call or just thinking about ending it and moving on.

MANAGEMENT TIP:

Top Sales Reps instinctively prepare themselves for a call and review a call. Since average sellers do not do this naturally, a manager can ask "Top Sales Rep Questions" of an average seller to help train that person to learn to ask similar questions himself/herself. Have a set of pre-call questions, and help the typical seller go through those questions before each call. Similarly, have a post-call or replay set of questions to review. With practice, the average seller can develop Top Sales Rep call planning and review habits.

Few sellers have a grasp of typical psychological terms for personality types. Even if they have been exposed to DISC systems or Myers-Briggs, few are likely to have mastered the system well enough to think about labeling their prospects with such terminology. However, every seller has his/her own label. Ask the seller to describe the person he/she just met, using whatever label he/she wants to use. They explore how best to interact with such a person. You can either teach them a more formal typing system or simply adapt to their labels and help them understand how better to use their own awareness of individual differences.

I worked with a Canadian call center where the TSRs labeled their prospects as Turtles, Friend-

*lies, Meanies, and "Get-a-Lifers" for people
who were slow, easy to engage, nasty, or eager
to take up a lot of time without buying, respec-
tively. The callers could make that label within
seconds of initiating the call. Each label had
behavior implications that allowed the manager
to teach callers how best to mirror or respond
to each type. By practicing how to adjust their
approach within seconds, the performance of
the call center's TSRs improved markedly.*

*Another client was an international manage-
ment consulting firm. They typically had to sell
projects to senior executives in an organization.
Fortunately, some of these prospects were high
profile individuals.*

*One Top Sales Rep in the firm knew he was go-
ing to be making a proposal to a high-profile
CEO. He found online videos of the CEO making some speeches. With that behavior sample,
he was able to adapt his sales presentation to
the prospect's NLP (neurolinguistic programming) mindset and NLP language preferences,
a sophisticated type labeling system.*

Chapter Nine:

SOCIAL INTELLIGENCE

In the previous chapter, it was mentioned that Top Sales Reps read others well. They know how to adapt to different personalities and styles.

They also demonstrate "Social Intelligence." This simply means they know how people fit into an organization, and they see how to use others as resources who can help them accomplish their goals. They know how to foster positive feelings from others. In other words, they know how to sell themselves to people within their organization and within client organizations–people who can make a difference in their success. They look for people with influence.

This is sometimes called "Use of Socialized Power (Boyatzis)" when used in the context of executive competencies. It is also contributes to what psychologists call "Conscientiousness", one of the Big Five psychological characteristics that impact success in the work place.

The path to Social intelligence includes an awareness of how people fit in the system and what they can contribute to the sales process. It also includes how to build relationships with key people through an expression of interest, gratitude, assistance, truthfulness, and a willingness to help others.

Some might call this characteristic "social maturity", although it is often quite narrow in its application. Many Top Sales Reps can be gracious and socially skilled with customers yet be a disruptive influence with peers and support staff back in the office. Assessing social intelligence as a trait is a challenge for this very reason. It can often have an on/off button for an individual, depending on the immediate setting.

Social Intelligence is different from Emotional Intelligence (EI). EI involves personal insight about one's own emotions as well as the insight into the feelings and concerns of others and using that insight to make good decisions. Social Intelligence, as seen in Top Sales Reps, relates to knowing who has influence, how that person fits in the system, and what that person can contribute to *my* success and *my* control of the situation. In other words, it can seem quite manipulative.

Top Sales Reps know how to use Social Intelligence well. They know how to build relationships with the right people and have them available as a needed. They know who can shortcut processes and bend the rules when needed. They know who can make a quick decision and who can make their life easier. With prospects or clients, they are apt to know who needs to be involved to get a decision made.

One of my clients was a Chicago company that hired field representatives to work with realtors to process new home mortgage applications. Their competitive advantage largely rested on their ability to quickly process a mortgage and make the broker happy with a quick response that helped close the home sale.

The routinely hired new college graduates for their training program. When a new sales candidate was hired, that person was expected to spend several weeks in the corporate office, where the applications were processed.

Within a few days, managers could predict who in the new class of college graduates was going to be a Top Sales Rep. The reason?

Future Top Sales Reps immediately realized they were working with the people who determined how fast the paperwork got done. If these people liked you and would process your paperwork, you could get the application processed faster and serve the outside brokers better thereby increasing your share of the business from any given broker. As a result, within a few days of starting their training pro-gram, the future Top Sales Reps would bring in morning coffee and donuts and start taking people out for pizza and lunch breaks. They recognized the value of these resources, and they wanted to win them over. They demon-strated "social intelligence."

INTERVIEW TIP:

Ask the candidate,

> *"Who has a major impact on whether you are successful or not?"*
>
> *"Who helps make your work easier?"*
>
> *"Give me an example of how that person(s) made a difference in a particular sale."*
>
> *"Give me another example."*
>
> *"How do you facilitate that relationship?"*

66

"Why do you think that person wants to help you?"

Listen for examples of Social Intelligence.

MANAGEMENT TIP:

Top Sales Reps know to find the key players in an organization who can make a difference. Help turn average sellers into more successful sellers by teaching about key relationships—who they need to know and how to build and maintain those relationships. Explain how certain people can make a difference in their success and why that relationship is important. Talk about how such relationships help the organization, but most important, how those relationships help the individual seller do his/her job better and with more success. If necessary, facilitate that relationship by introducing key people and encouraging interaction. Provide similar direction and insight about key relationships in customer and prospect organizations. Open doors for your sellers and guide them in relationship building and relationship maintenance.

Chapter Ten:

REFERRAL REQUESTS

Finding new business is always a challenge for any seller. Average sellers are often most content in businesses that allow them to be order-takers or account managers—building relationships with a portfolio of accounts and servicing those accounts exclusively. When these average sellers are asked to generate new business, they are often frustrated. They often do not know how to begin a cold call, and they are suddenly looking at more rejection than they have ever experienced. Their energy drops and their effectiveness suffers.

No one really likes cold calls. No one likes getting rejected. Top Sales Reps are as frustrated by rejection as anyone else. But they also are driven to find efficient ways to meet their end goal. Top Sales Reps are practical. They want to be successful.

So Top Sales Reps do what practically any Sales Manager will tell you to do: ask an existing customer to make a referral! They know that asking for a referral is much more efficient than filling a sales funnel with real cold calls. When someone can say, *"I just sold a new car to Frank*

Jones, and he said you might appreciate the kind of deal I gave him," that call is no longer so cold. It is a more practical and efficient way to get new business.

When a customer buys something, he/she is probably going to feel better about that decision *at that time* than at any other time. Top Sales Reps realize this fact. When the deal is closed, they ask for a referral: *"You obviously decided this was a good decision for you. Do you know anyone else who might benefit from the same choice?"* It is much easier and more productive to fill a funnel with referrals than with cold leads.

What many Sales Managers may not realize is that the act of *asking* is a challenge for the average seller. The average seller is happy with the sale. It is a great feeling. Why risk wrecking that good feeling by asking for something else and getting rejected?

Average sellers often suffer from a single major weakness: They do not want to *ask* for anything. Psychologically, this makes some sense. If you do not ask for anything, you will not get rejected. In practice, this means that the average seller may resist asking for business, asking for money, and even asking for a referral. Some say weak sellers suffer from being uncomfortable talking about money, but it seems the issue may be deeper. The discomfort may be due to the fear of rejection when asking for anything. Top Sales Reps ask for business…and for re-ferrals.

INTERVIEW TIP:

Ask the candidate,

> *"What percent of your new sales last year came from referrals by existing customers?"*

> *"Think about your last (specific) sale…what did you sell? Did that customer give you a referral? Why/Why not?" (Listen to see if they asked.)*

> *"What customer has given you the most or best referrals?"*

> *"Give me an example of your following up on a referral from an existing customer. What did you say? Did you get a new sale?"*

> *"How long do you typically wait after a customer signs an agreement to ask that customer for a referral?"*

MANAGEMENT TIP:

If you want a new behavior, measure it. Measure and post the number of referrals a seller receives from existing customers. Track how many referrals lead to a sale.

Emphasize and reward the number of referrals, not the specific sales results. The sales will come if the referrals are obtained.

With average sellers, role-play how to ask for a referral. Practice several scenarios until the seller can find a "script" that feels comfortable. This will take some time and a lot of practice. If you know a seller is going to see a customer and close the sale during that meeting, rehearse how to ask that customer for referrals.

Chapter Eleven:

MIRRORING BEHAVIOR

NLP (neurolinguistic programming) is a collection of observations and subsequent modeling behaviors that can help someone sell more effectively. It is a set of behaviors that allow a person to sell himself/herself quickly. NLP skills range from using different metaphors to adapting language style to fit the prospect or customer. (See The Unfair Advantage: Sell with NLP!)

Top Sales Reps tend to use one such skill—"Mirroring"— without realizing they are doing so. In fact, teaching Top Sales Reps to mirror can disrupt their natural style initially. They usually do this behavior naturally and unconsciously.

Mirroring is simply copying some aspect of another individual. Sometimes you can mirror voice characteristics such as loudness or speed of talking. You can also mirror physical posturing and gestures.

Top Sales Reps mirror naturally. They typically match the posture or stance of the person on whom they are calling. Sometimes they will unconsciously match the accent of their customer. They will adapt to the customer's environment and match words or phrases that are part of the customer's or prospect's world.

Mirroring enables a Top Sales Rep to establish rapport and put people at ease. When a Top Sales Rep mirrors a prospect, the prospect is more apt to trust the seller and be less wary about what is said. Top Sales Reps learn much more from prospects and customers when they also mirror behaviors.

I once heard a Top Sales Rep talking on the phone with a customer. His voice quickly changed and he suddenly had a slight Southern accent.

When he hung up, he said, "Wow. I have got to stop doing that!"

I asked, "Stop doing what?"

He said, "Mimicking. I don't know why I do it, but I suddenly realize I am talking like my customer."

He did not realize that such a talent was one reason he was a Top Sales Rep.

INTERVIEW TIP:

The interview is a selling environment. The candidate is trying to sell you. Notice if he/she makes any attempt to mirror you. Notice if there is an attempt to mirror your initial posture. Does the candidate pick up on words you use in a question or comment and repeat the exact words? Does the candidate match your speed of talk as you ask a question?

Interviews are tough places to assess a candidate's ability to mirror. This is especially true, because a good interviewer should be *mirroring the candidate* to help him/her relax and be more open. But watch the early initial phase of the interview to see if the candidate does any mirroring.

You can also ask,

> *"When you meet a new prospect, how do you adjust your style of presenting?"*

> *"How do you know when a prospect is comfortable with you? How do you help make this process occur?"*

Listen to see if the candidate has a conscious awareness of mirroring. Awareness is not necessary if he/she does it naturally, however.

Be aware that as the interview progresses, you may succeed in making a psychological connection with the candidate. If this occurs, you may notice he/she copies your movements or gestures, such as scratching your nose or straightening your hair. This does not mean the candidate uses mirroring to help sell. It simply means you have successfully established rapport with the candidate. You are leading, and the candidate is following. Well done.

MANAGEMENT TIP:

Mirroring can be taught. When teaching mirroring, however, be certain that the seller understands the risk in being noticed. Teach how to pause before matching physical posture changes, for instance. Simply repeating a word or phrase someone uses is another easy way to mirror. Mirroring is simply a way of operationalizing an old adage: People most like people most like themselves.

Chapter Twelve:

FINAL THOUGHTS ON MANAGING TOP SALES REPS

Are Top Sales Reps born or developed? It does not really matter what you believe. The fact is: Top Sales Reps are different. If you understand the differences, you can try to find the "natural" Top Sales Rep or you can hire talent and train the person how to think and act like a Top Sales Rep.

If you are lucky enough to have some Top Sales Reps on your sales team, realize that you must treat them differently. They have different needs. As a Top Sales Rep recently told me, *"I want insights and information, not answers."* He added, he has never been interested in empty praise, but he appreciates specific acknowledgment. *"(I) never enjoyed being singled out as the 'best', but if I'm not included in the 'Best of...' list, you've lost me."* They need different kinds of attention from you. Be prepared to feed that animal, and you will benefit from their skills and experience. You want to keep that Top Sales Rep happy.

Do not promote the Top Sales Rep to a manager role. Why would you want to lose a producer and create a mediocre manager? Be flexible with your compensation plan so that a Top Sales Rep's earnings continue to grow without having to move to a new position or a new company. Adapt the sales territory or product line to match the seller. Make sure your compensation to a Top Sales Rep is fair and seen as fair by that seller.

Do not be tempted to put a Top Sales Rep in a dead territory with the hope of revitalizing the territory. The loss of control as well as the loss of status will be damaging to the seller's self-esteem and confidence. Add slowly to the job of the Top Sales Rep, or you will damage the delicate balance that is a Top Sales Rep's personality.

One size management does not fit everyone. You may want your sales team to fill out call reports or submit price proposals in a specific way. But Top Sales Reps may have to be given a "get out of jail free" card at times. Be willing to be flexible. If a Top Sales Rep is producing outstanding results, do you really need to enforce your rules with everyone? Bend them a bit if the results justify making an exception. As a Top Sales Rep told me, *"I don't need to be motivated; just don't demotivate me."*

Give the Top Sales Rep what he/she needs. Put up with their controlling behavior. Help remove roadblocks.

Respect the fears that Top Sales Reps have, and avoid giving selling advice. Give them an open road to sell. Help them be successful if they are in a slump. Everyone wins. And if an average seller complains, the solution is obvious: become a Top Sales Rep.

ADDENDUM

This first draft of this book was completed in the early summer of 2015. Within a few days of it being submitted for publication, an article appeared in the Journal of Applied Psychology, Volume 100. This is a publication affiliated with the American Psychological Association. The article was titled, "Stargazing: An Integrative Conceptual Review, Theoretical Reconciliation, and Extension for Star Employee Research" by Matthew Call, Anthony Nyberg, and Sherry Thatcher of the University of South Carolina.

To my delight, their research tracked very closely the observations and conclusions I drew in this book from my years of working with sales professionals.

They analyzed 75 research articles on stars and high performers. They defined a star as someone who demonstrates prolonged high performance, visibility, and relevant social capital (influence and relationships "that provide access to information, resources, and opportunities"), or in other words, a Top Sales Rep. Their conclusions from studying the psychological research on "stars" included the following:

1. A "star" refers to "relative" performance, not actual levels. In other words, a top performer tends to seek to be best in his/her group, but the actual performance may not always be considered "top" if using a different set of criteria. This is consistent with the old joke paraphrased in the book about not needing to outrun a bear but only outrun the other campers.

2. Stars engage in "deliberate practice". This is similar to "grit" discussed in the book. The authors wrote, "Gritty individuals are likely to persevere and engage in the practice necessary to become disproportionately high performers."

3. The article also identified that stars have a unique drive to learn. "'Learning goal orientation' is particularly critical for stars," they wrote.

4. The researchers recognized that stars need recognition and validation. As they wrote, "a desire for self-enhancement motivates visibility (and performance)". Yet, they wrote, "Some top performers may prefer to avoid the scrutiny and expectations that accompany public attention." This is consistent with my observation that Top Sales Reps often do not like awards and ceremonies.

5. The authors' research also acknowledged the value of sharing information about employee performance. Such public posting of results can provide validation to a seller,

but they also warn it can lead to jealousy and inflated self-assessment with some sellers.

6. The research recognized that stars need to be treated in a special way. "While we teach managers to avoid preferential treatment, this counsel might be inappropriate when managing stars...high performing employees are also more sensitive to pay growth and perceived pay for performance. Thus, if stars behave like high performers, when they perceive themselves receiving low pay relative to their performance, they are more likely than low performers to leave the organization."

7. As mentioned in my observations, a manager can be a valuable asset to a Top Sales Rep by helping the seller to build relationships with key people, inside and outside the organization. The research analyzed in the journal found the same to be true. "(Organizations) should also manage the star's social network, because an abundance of ties increases the likelihood of a star's retention."

It is nice to have research mirror the insight gained from experience. It proves that, in psychology, there is room for both researchers and practitioners, and the public wins when we work together.

Duane Lakin, Ph.D.
Lakin Associates

For over 35 years, Dr. Lakin has been a management psychologist, helping business executives reduce surprises when hiring or promoting people. Through a process of interviewing and testing, he identifies the strengths and weaknesses of individuals in the business setting--whether it is a manager candidate or a current manager or even team of people. He also trains and coaches individuals and teams to help them see how to be more effective.

His interest in Top Sales Reps has developed as a result of his many years of selecting, coaching, listening to, and observing sales people as they work, grow, and sometimes struggle. He has also seen the challenges that sales managers often face when working with Top Sales Reps. He knows the value of knowing how to work with and nurture those Top Sales Reps.

In addition to his assessment service, Dr. Lakin works with professionals in many fields in the practical application of what is called Neurolinguistic Programming (NLP) techniques for sales and management. His workshop, *The Unfair Advantage—Sell with NLP!* has been seen by representatives of over 750 companies in the U.S., U.K., Russia, Hungary, Italy, and Canada. His research and consulting in NLP applications to telemarketing are unique in the industry. He has trained managers from companies such as Xerox, PacBell, Andersen Consulting, American General, Cable and Wireless, Hewlett Packard, GE, and many others. He has written or contributed to articles in *Selling Power, HR Magazine, Production and Inventory Management,* and *Sales and Marketing Excellence.* He has also talked to many professional organizations on NLP as well as interview skills. He is a recipient of the "TEC 200" and "Vistage 100 Achievement Award" designations for outstanding resource speakers to TEC (now called Vistage). He is a member of the American Psychological Association.

His book, *The Unfair Advantage: Sell with NLP!,* is consistently a top rated book on NLP for sales. You can read the reviews at Amazon.com and elsewhere on the Internet. It has been translated and published in Romanian, Polish and Spanish languages. An audio version of the book is available from iTunes Store, and a video of the live workshop is also available.

His more recent book, *The Unfair Advantage: Sell with NLP! for Inside Sales Professionals"* is available through Amazon, iTunes Store, and other distributors. For more information, go to the website SellWithNLP.com or visit LinkedIn.

Lakin Associates
630-871-2996
www.lakinassociates.com
www.SellWithNLP.com
drlakin@lakinassociates.com

See Dr. Lakin's profile on:
Linked in.